THE HUMAN BODY IN 3D

THE EAR IN 3D

rosen publishing's

rosen central

NICHOLAS FAULKNER
AND JOSEPHA SHERMAN

Published in 2016 by The Rosen Publishing Group, Inc.
29 East 21st Street, New York, NY 10010

First Edition

Library of Congress Cataloging-in-Publication Data

Faulkner, Nicholas.
The ear in 3D/Nicholas Faulkner and Josepha Sherman.—First edition.
    pages cm—(The human body in 3D)
Includes bibliographical references and index.
ISBN 978-1-4994-3585-6 (library bound)—ISBN 978-1-4994-3587-0 (pbk.)—
ISBN 978-1-4994-3588-7 (6-pack)
1. Ear—Juvenile literature. 2. Hearing—Juvenile literature. I. Sherman, Josepha. II. Title.
QP462.2.F38 2016
612.8'54—dc23

2015000238

Manufactured in the United States of America

CONTENTS

INTRODUCTION

The ear, surprisingly, is one of the most complex and fascinating systems in the human body. While it is obviously meant for hearing, it also serves the functions of maintaining balance, allowing a person to stand, turn, and walk. So if you imagine life without these critical parts of the body, we not only wouldn't be able to hear we wouldn't be able to have the bodily mobility we're used to.

This resource takes us into the anatomy and function of the ear. The outer portion, called the auricle, captures sound, almost like a catcher's mitt. Sound then travels to the inner ear, which is much more complex and sensitive. It is here where sound waves are transmitted into signals that our brains can understand. This is also where our ears communicate with our brains so that we can maintain our balance and coordination.

In addition to helping us maintain balance, the ear is responsible for coordinating eye and head movement. When you move your head, fluid in the ear moves as well, stirring tiny hairs within the ear, sending a signal to the brain. Much of our physical coordination has to do with the ear.

For some animals, the ears also serve as a means of communication. Depending on the way they move their ears, animals might be saying certain things. A dog, for instance, will flatten

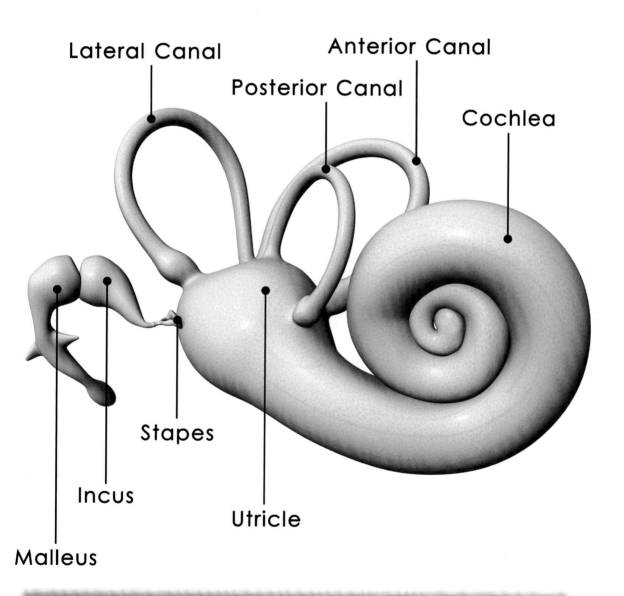

Lateral Canal

Anterior Canal

Posterior Canal

Cochlea

Stapes

Incus

Utricle

Malleus

The inner ear has many delicate and complex parts. Doctors and scientists are continuing to learn about the ear's makeup and how we hear.

his ears if he's angry. Throughout the animal kingdom, there are many ways that the ears communicate to others.

With such a complex and delicate system, many problems can arise with the ear as well, such as hearing loss and loss of balance. It wasn't until recently, though, that doctors and scientists developed the technology to correct hearing loss in the form of hearing aids and other devices. More and more of these products are coming on the market every year as we continue to learn about how the ear communicates with the brain.

Very little was known about the workings of the inner ear until recently. Today, we know that hearing disorders are not just the result of listening to loud music or being exposed to a sudden loud noise. There are congenital conditions, meaning the person was born with it, and acquired conditions, meaning that they were a result of an outside occurrence. By better understanding the condition and its cause, doctors are better equipped to repair hearing damage, even giving hearing to those who never before heard a single sound. Imagine that, the experience of hearing sound for the very first time.

This resource examines all aspects of the ear from the outside in. You will learn exactly how the ear works with 3D images of the anatomy of the ear. The imagery will help you visualize the complex structure of the ear.

CHAPTER ONE

THE EAR UP CLOSE

Our ears are not just for hearing—or for hanging earrings! It is a complex part of the body, more so than we might imagine. The whole outer ear is called the auricle, which means "ear" in Latin. The bendable segment is the pinna, from the Latin word that means "leaf," because it looks something like a leaf. (You can see a clearer leaf-shape in the ear of an animal like the dog or horse.) Latin, by the way, is the usual language used in science. At one time it was the language that all scholars held in common, and every scientist understood it.

The auricle is made of a thin plate of cartilage tightly covered by skin. Cartilage is a form of connective tissue, more flexible and compressible than bone. The ear is attached to the side of the head by several small muscles, most of which serve no other use and have no strength, although the occasional person can "wiggle" his or her ears with them.

HUMAN VS. ANIMAL EARS

Humans rely more on sight than on hearing. But animals that depend on hearing to warn them of predators or alert them to prey have large, pointed ears that "cup" sound. Their ear muscles are better developed than those in humans, letting them turn their ears in all directions to locate a specific noise.

Animals with mobile ears also use them as part of their "language." A curious dog will prick his ears straight up—but he'll flatten his ears back if he's angry. And a bored or sleepy dog will just let his ears flop.

THE OUTER EAR

The curve of the outer ear, the portion of the ear furthest from the ear's attachment to the head, is known as the helix. This name comes to us through Latin from the Greek word for "curve" or "folding in." The edge of the outer curve is the crux of the helix, from the Latin for "cross," meaning the "main point" of the helix. Follow the curve down to the bottom of the ear, and there is the fleshy lobule, more commonly known as the ear lobe. Different people have different lengths and shapes to their ear lobes, but there doesn't seem to be any scientific reason for the variations. The lobule plays no role in hearing.

Curving in from the helix at the top of the ear is what seems to be a true canal. But the indentation quickly ends in a small bowl. In fact, it barely seems to be worth the name of

The outer ear serves as a device for "catching" sound waves. It acts as a cup and directs sounds into the ear canal.

canal at all, but its scientific name is the helix canal. The lower side of the helix canal "bowl," which is lower than the crux of the helix, is named the antihelix, meaning that it's an opposite of the true helix.

Below the antihelix are the concha and the cavum of concha. *Concha* is Latin for "shell," and that part of the ear really does look something like a shell, and *cavum* means exactly what it seems—this is the start of the "cave" of the ear canal. It has the more scientific name of the external auditory canal, or the external auditory meatus. *Meatus* is the Latin word for a natural opening.

THOMAS SYDENHAM

English physician Thomas Sydenham (1624–1689) was one of the most important radical medical reformers of the seventeenth century. Because of his politics, his influence during his lifetime was not great. Eventually, however, he came to be known as the English Hippocrates. Sydenham was born into a family of wealthy gentry, but he sided with Oliver Cromwell and against King Charles I in the English Civil War (1642–1651). Cromwell's supporters wanted to reduce the power of the English king and increase the power of the English Parliament. Sydenham became a captain in the parliamentary army and fought in several fierce battles. His military career interrupted his education. He did not get his master's degree until 1648, and he did not begin practicing medicine until 1656.

It was in fact his inability to advance himself in public life that made Sydenham turn to medicine. After the defeat of Cromwell and the restoration of King Charles II, there was no room in politics or society for people with antimonarchist views. So Sydenham set up a practice in London and applied his reformer's passion to medical science. Sydenham agreed with the ancient Greek physician Hippocrates (460–377 BCE) that observation and experience counted for more than theory. He insisted upon the need to observe patients and their symptoms carefully and to keep detailed case histories.

The result of all this careful observation and recording of symptoms was the publication of *Medical Observations*, in which Sydenham described precisely the effects of diseases he had studied in London from 1661 to 1675. This was the first accurate description of such diseases as measles, dysentery, gout, and cholera. By carefully discriminating between symptoms, Sydenham was able to identify a new disease, scarlet fever. Unfortunately, Sydenham also adopted Hippocrates's belief that diseases were caused by imbalances in the four "humours": blood, phlegm, black bile, and yellow bile. At the time of Hippocrates, such a theory was an advance over the ancient notion that the gods caused illnesses because it advanced the idea of natural causes for disease. Inaccurate though the theory was, it was all that Sydenham had to work with. The germ theory of disease would not be introduced until the nineteenth century. In spite of this, Sydenham is considered the founder of modern clinical medicine and epidemiology, the science of disease control in populations. His studies of epidemics would remain the best knowledge available to doctors until the work of Louis Pasteur (1822–1895).

Sydenham was also the first doctor to use laudanum, an opium derivative, to relieve pain. He promoted the use of cinchona bark, which contains quinine, to treat malaria. He used iron to treat patients suffering from anemia. He belonged to a small group of doctors and scientists who, even before the industrial and scientific revolutions of the eighteenth century, tried to turn medical science away from its dependence upon ancient authorities.

MOVING INSIDE THE EAR

The outer ear is as much as can be seen of the ear with the eye alone. But the external auditory canal continues inward for a little over an inch. The canal is lined all the way with fine hairs pointing outward and has modified sweat glands that produce cerumen, or earwax. Both are there to keep foreign objects, such as insects, out of the ear.

The auditory canal ends at the tympanic membrane. This is another name that should be easily understood by anyone who knows that the formal word for drums is tympani. The tympanic membrane is a thin strip of skin that looks like the head of a drum—in fact, its common name is the eardrum. Richly filled with nerve endings and tiny blood vessels, it's extremely sensitive to noise and pain, and can be relatively easily damaged. Many injuries to the eardrum will heal themselves without leaving a loss of hearing, but it's better to be careful. When cleaning out an ear, for instance, never use

There are many components to the ear, including countless channels, nerve endings, and blood vessels, which are all very sensitive.

anything that might push earwax—or anything else—against the membrane.

THE MIDDLE EAR

Beyond the thin membrane of the eardrum lies the air-filled cavity of the middle ear and the loosely connected sections of the ossicular chain. The word *ossicular* is the Latin term for "bony." An ossicular chain is exactly what the middle ear holds: a linking of three tiny bones. All three get their names from their appearances. The first bone is the malleus, which is Latin for "hammer." The second bone is the incus, which is Latin for "anvil," and the third and furthest in from the middle ear is the stapes, which means the "stirrup." While you need a little imagination to see a hammer or an anvil in the first two bones, the stapes really does look the most like its namesake, down to the flat base of the stapes that looks very much like the base of an English saddle's stirrup.

Also found in the middle ear is one end of the Eustachian tube, which

This 3D rendering shows the outer ear transposed on the middle and inner ear, giving a sense of the regions' relative sizes.

is made up of bone and cartilage and lined with tiny hair cells called cilia. The other end of the Eustachian tube is attached to the pharynx. This is the cavity at the back of the mouth that leads down into the esophagus, which is more commonly known as the windpipe, and which lets us breath through our mouths as well as our noses. Not every mammal has this opening. The horse, for instance, does not—and as a result can't breathe through its mouth.

The Eustachian tube lets fluid flow properly down the throat, and it keeps the pressure equal on both sides of the eardrum. It also allows excess fluid to drain out of the middle ear and opens wide to let air flow in or out of it three or four times during a yawn, a chew, or a swallow.

THE INNER EAR

The base of the stapes rests against the main structure of the inner ear, the cochlea. This and the whole inner ear comprise a complex system

Sound waves enter the outer ear and travel to the eardrum. The vibrations are then sent to three tiny bones in the middle ear and then to the inner ear.

of fluid-filled tubes and sacs that is called the bony labyrinth, and it really does look like one big maze.

But for all its complexity, the cochlea is tiny, no bigger than the very tip of a little finger. The word *cochlea* means "snail" in

Though the middle and inner ear are made up of a vast and complex system of passageways, including the snail-like cochlea to the right, the entire structure is tiny.

Latin, and that's roughly what it looks like: a snail facing toward the middle ear, but one with three looping tubes coming out of its head. About where the eye would be on the snail is the oval or vesticular window, made of a thin, vibrating membrane. The three tubes that come up and loop down again to the cochlea are, starting with the one closest to the middle ear, the lateral semicircular canal, the posterior semicircular canal, and the anterior semicircular canal. They are filled with fluid and lined, like the Eustachian tube, with cilia. What looks like the snail's body is the coiled-up cochlear nerve. Resting on the "snail's back" is the vestibular nerve. This is a segment of the acoustic nerve, one of the eight cranial nerves of the brain.

CHAPTER TWO

HOW WE HEAR AND MAINTAIN BALANCE

While we might first think of the ear as a means by which we hear, it also has another important function. Not only does it let someone hear, the ear also allows that person to stand, turn, and walk. How the ear achieves all this is a process that's both amazingly complex and amazingly swift and accurate.

The process of hearing, of course, has to begin with a sound, such as the ringing of a phone. Sound is produced when an action, such as that telephone ringing, sets air molecules vibrating. The vibrations, in turn, become sound waves. As anyone who has ever swum underwater or listened to recordings of whale "songs" knows, sound waves can travel through air or water and still be heard. Though of course we can't see a sound wave, it is as real as an ocean wave, though it looks a little different. Instead of waving up and down, sound waves consist of regions of compressed, or tightly packed, air molecules, followed by regions where the

Sound waves are captured by the outer ear and directed into the auditory canal. They then vibrate the tympanic membrane and move through the ossicular chain.

air molecules are more thinly packed. The distance between two tightly packed regions is called the wavelength. The rate at which these tightly packed regions move past a fixed point is called the frequency. The molecules themselves don't change position much. The wave, or disturbance, that passes through the air molecules is energy.

HOW SOUND TRAVELS

While sound can travel through both air and water, it cannot travel through a vacuum. Space is, of course, a vacuum. When moviemakers first started to film science fiction, they discovered something funny about the human ear and mind. We are conditioned to hear something move, especially something that's supposed to be whizzing by at great speed. We also expect an explosion to make a loud noise. Without sound, the excitement of a high-speed chase in outer space was missing, and the shock of an exploding planet just wasn't shocking enough. The moviemakers had to add sound effects to their movies to make spaceships roar across the screen and explosions really go "boom!"

UNDERSTANDING SOUND WAVES

The sound wave is caught and "cupped" by the curve of the outer ear, the external auricle, and funneled toward the ear canal, down which it travels until it reaches the tympanic membrane, the eardrum. The sound wave "strikes" the membrane and is transformed into vibrations in the eardrum. This is the same thing that happens, by the way, when sound waves strike a microphone and cause its artificial membrane to vibrate.

But not all wave frequencies can make the human eardrum vibrate. We can't, for instance, hear sounds at too high a frequency because the sound waves travel one after another too swiftly to give the membrane a chance to vibrate. Those extremely fast

Sound waves travel through the small and delicate structures of the middle and inner ear.

frequencies are called ultrasonic. Some mammals, such as dogs and bats, have specialized ear structures and can hear them, but we cannot. The ear's perception of sound wave frequency is called pitch: the greater the frequency, the higher the pitch.

STUDYING THE EAR

For centuries, nobody knew that the structure of the ear was so complicated. But in the seventeenth century, scientists began making careful studies of the ear. They assumed, though, that the inner ear had only the function of hearing and weren't sure what part of that function the semicircular canals served. It wasn't until French scientist Marie-Jean-Pierre Flourens began working with pigeons in 1824 that he discovered that the ear is also responsible for giving us balance. It wasn't until the end of that century that his findings were internationally accepted. Science sometimes hears only what it wants to hear.

Another factor in the proper transmission of the sound wave is its intensity. If it's too faint, too soft, like that created by a whisper or from something far away, it barely causes a vibration of the eardrum. If it's too intense a sound wave, it causes genuine pain. We say that such painful sounds are too loud. We can also measure them in a scale using units of measurement called decibels. A jet engine at full throttle, for instance, will produce far more decibels, 130, than normal conversation, which produces

Though scientists have been studying the ear for centuries, there is still much to learn about how we hear. This nineteenth century historical anatomical artwork of a human ear shows the outer and internal structure of the ear.

fifty to sixty decibels. A rock concert, incidentally, produces about 100 decibels. The threshold of pain is at about 140 decibels.

Those sound waves that are within the normal human range of hearing succeed in creating vibrations in the membrane that are passed inward to the middle ear. The vibrations strike the handle of the malleus, the hammer that's the first bone in the ossicular chain. The vibrations speed to the head of the malleus and from it to the incus, the anvil. The vibrations are passed along to the stapes, the stirrup, which swings back and forth, passing them in turn to the oval window of the cochlea and the organ of Corti within the cochlea. Now the sound vibrations are transformed to liquid vibrations through the cochlea's fluid. They are analyzed, sorted, and transformed again, this time into neural impulses that travel to the brain. The brain translates the sound as that of a ringing phone. What's more, the angle at which the sound waves strike the outer ear gives the brain clues as to the telephone's location.

It's truly astonishing that so much analysis and translation takes place in far less time than a second. What's more, the ear and

The ear, positioned just below the temporal lobe (yellow region), works with the brain to convert sound waves into signals that you can understand.

brain are constantly processing sounds, and processing many sounds at the same time, and almost never making a mistake. The system isn't perfect, of course, since the brain can't identify something the ear hasn't heard before. We can get confused if the telephone sounds too much like the doorbell. But we don't make mistakes about the sounds that are important to us. The sounds of a baby crying or a fire alarm clanging will create instant recognition.

THE EAR AND BALANCE

The ear serves another function that's every bit as important as hearing, and that's providing the body with its balance. Without the inner ear, it would be impossible for someone to even stand without falling over, let alone to walk or bend or turn. To easily test the truth of that statement, try twirling about like a child until you are dizzy, then try to walk. In addition, the inner ear is responsible for coordinating eye movement, as well as eye and head movement.

It's the vestibular system within the inner ear that actually does the work. The three semicircular canals on the "head" of the "snail" deal with keeping the body stable when it turns. Whenever the body or head moves, the fluid in the semicircular canals moves as well, stirring like water in a pipe. As it moves, the fluid also stirs the tiny hair cells, the neural filaments that line the semicircular canals and are linked to the acoustic nerve.

The ear works with the rest of the human anatomy, including your muscle and nervous system, to help you maintain balance.

These neural hair cells signal to the brain that the body or head has moved.

Meanwhile, two tiny membranous sacs within the inner ear, the smaller saccule and the larger utricle, contain the

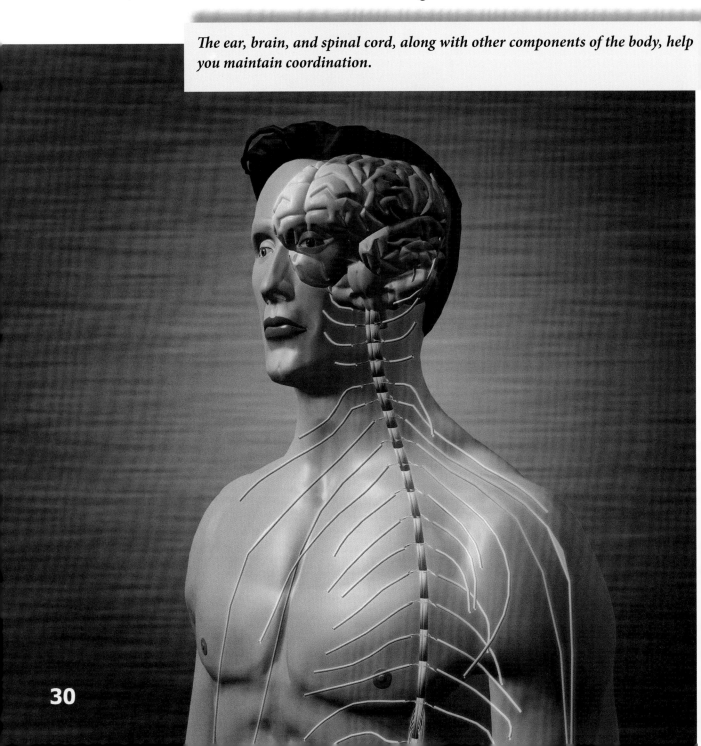

The ear, brain, and spinal cord, along with other components of the body, help you maintain coordination.

same type of hair cells, neural filaments that link up to the acoustic nerve. In this case, they're disturbed only when the body moves forward or backward, stirred one way if it goes forward and the other way if it backs up. Then the hair cells signal to the brain that the body is moving, and which way it's going.

There's one more amazing fact about balance and hearing. They are both the result of the ear and the brain working in partnership—it's work on a "24/7" basis and work of which we're not even aware.

CHAPTER THREE

UNDERSTANDING HEARING DISORDERS

The ear is a wonderfully complex system. But as with any part of the body that has many mechanisms, things can go wrong, such as hearing disorders, among other things.

A hearing disorder may be present from birth. In that case, it's called congenital. If it occurs after birth, the disorder is called acquired. Some doctors further subdivide acquired hearing disorder into pre-lingual (happening before a child learns to speak) and post-lingual (happening after a child learns to speak).

Genetic problems are responsible for about half of all the cases of congenital hearing loss. In fact, research into the human genome, the entire DNA "blueprint" of the human body, has revealed more than one "deafness gene" that may be responsible for hereditary deafness. Often, the problem comes from what is known as a recessive gene. Both parent may have perfectly normal hearing, yet carry a recessive "deafness gene" without

Hearing disorders can strike any region of the ear, including deep inside the middle and inner regions.

realizing it. Their child would then have a 25 percent chance of inheriting both recessive "deafness genes" and being born with a hearing loss. There are also some genetic syndromes that often include hearing problems, such as Down syndrome or fetal alcohol syndrome.

Some ear disorders strike the hair cells inside of the cochlea.

In addition, accidental exposure to harmful chemicals or environmental hazards can damage the genes of a developing embryo. Other problems can include infections such as German measles, which can be passed to the embryo, and premature birth, which means that the ear structure may not have had a chance to develop properly.

CONGENITAL CONDITIONS

Genetic deformation of the outer ear is called congenital microtia. The defect can range from something as minor as a missing fold of the helix, the edge of the outer ear, to a completely missing external ear. The shape of a malformed outer ear may block sound to the inner ear.

Congenital atresia means that there is no external ear canal. In these cases, a bony plate blocks the middle ear, often completely. What's worse is that congenital atresia is almost always

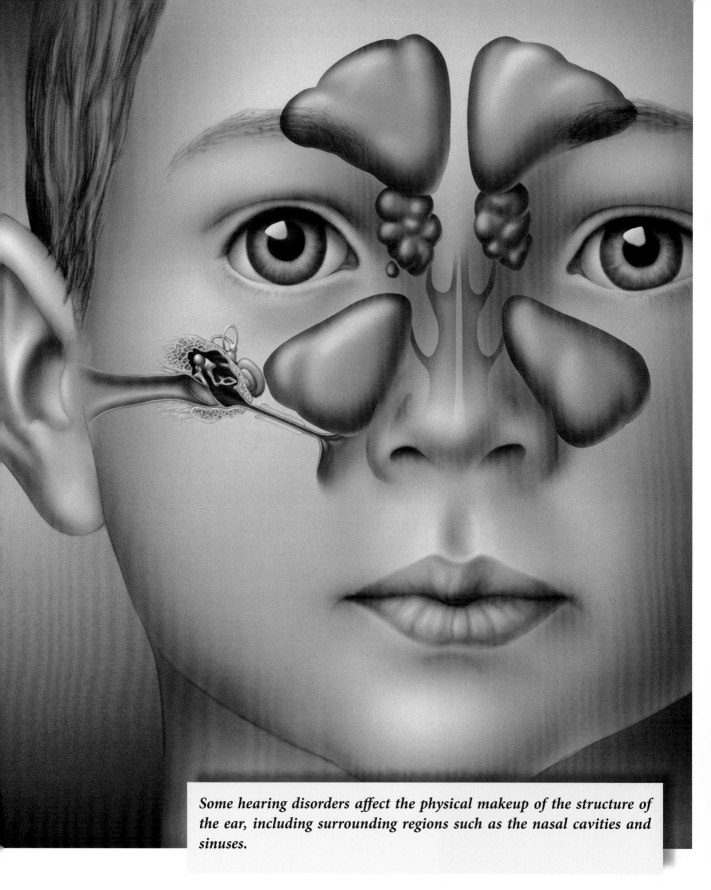

Some hearing disorders affect the physical makeup of the structure of the ear, including surrounding regions such as the nasal cavities and sinuses.

accompanied by malformations of the middle ear bones as well. For instance, sometimes the malleus or the stapes are fused to other bones so that they can't move freely and transmit vibrations properly. In milder forms of atresia, the ear canal may exist but be much more narrow than normal, allowing less of the sound wave to enter the ear.

ACQUIRED HEARING LOSS

The second type of hearing disorder is called acquired hearing loss. This is generally not related to any genetic problems. Acquired hearing loss is something that can happen to someone at any stage of his or her life and has several possible causes, ranging from illness to injury.

The most common illness to affect the ear is called otitis media: the common ear infection known to almost every child. Indeed, over 50 percent of children will have suffered an ear infection by the age of one. The reason for this is the fact that in children the Eustachian tube isn't as fully grown or slanted as it becomes in adults. This means that a child's ear is much more susceptible to infections. The middle ear becomes filled with fluid, and sound vibrations aren't passed along as efficiently. Sound becomes unclear or muffled. There can even be painful pressure put on the eardrum. Usually, the condition is temporary, and hearing clears up as soon as the infection is healed. But if ear infections are too common or too severe, they can damage the eardrum, or the bones and nerve. This causes a permanent

Fluid buildup inside the inner ear can lead to acquired hearing disorders, such as ear infections.

hearing loss. Other diseases that can cause permanent damage to the inner and middle ear include measles, mumps, and meningitis.

In addition to diseases creating problems for the ear, cures for other, non-hearing related diseases might also cause hearing harm. Some medicines, while perfectly harmless to hearing if used properly, become dangerous to the ear if they are used for long periods or time or taken in overly large doses. They can create enough fluid build-up in the inner and middle ear to cause permanent hearing loss. These medicines include very high doses of aspirin and some common antibiotics, including erythromycin and streptomycin.

A separate category of hearing problem is called tinnitus, which is a high-pitched and annoying ringing or buzzing sound inside the ear. Unfortunately, it has many possible causes, including exposure to loud noise, an ear infection, allergies, or seemingly no obvious reason at all. Sometimes tinnitus stops on its own, but sometimes it lasts long enough to badly interfere with sufferers' lives.

When tinnitus is accompanied by symptoms such as dizziness, nausea, and distorted hearing, it is called Meniere's disease. This disease involves the buildup of excessive fluid in the canals of the inner ear and is a common cause of hearing loss.

Yet another form of acquired hearing loss is called presbycusia, or age-related hearing loss. This condition begins with a loss of higher-frequency sounds, often while the person is in his or her 40s, and gradually worsens over the years as the

TEMPORARY THRESHOLD SHIFT

A teenaged girl who had attended a long rock concert the night before reported that a day later she still felt as though she had cotton in her ears, which were persistently ringing. It took several days for her hearing to return completely to normal. And former president Bill Clinton wears a small hearing aid to treat his minimal hearing loss, which is due to, as he freely admits, attending too many rock concerts in his teens.

What happened to the teen is called a "temporary threshold shift," in which the hair cells of the cochlea malfunction but recover. Clinton wasn't so lucky. In his case, too many repeated episodes of such shifts caused a permanent threshold shift from which the hair cells couldn't recover.

normal course of everyday life slowly wears down the hair cells of the cochlea. It's more common in men than women and possibly has a hereditary link.

As we age, the components of the ear wear down just like the rest of our bodies. The more delicate structures, such as inside the cochlear duct, are particularly vulnerable.

HEARING LOSS FROM INJURIES

Injuries form the second category of acquired hearing loss. Someone who has suffered a major head injury, such as the result of a car crash or too violent a tackle in football, may find

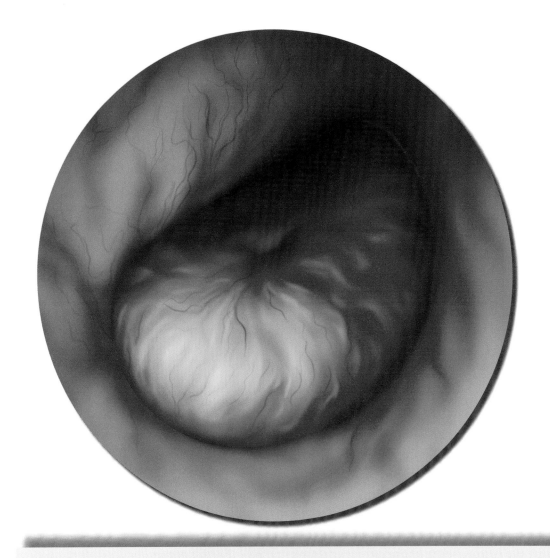

Hearing loss can result from a variety of factors, ranging from the common ear infection (shown here) to serious head injuries.

that his or her injury includes damage to the ear, ranging from a ruptured—or torn—eardrum to fractures of the ear's bones. In addition, too vigorous probing of the ear canal with a Q-tip or other object can puncture the eardrum, as can too panicky an attempt to remove an insect. Far safer to let the insect leave by itself or to wash out the ear with warm water.

Sudden sharp, loud noises also do damage. People too close to exploding firecrackers or other explosions often suffer hearing loss, temporary or, if they're unlucky enough to have an eardrum ruptured by the force of the blast, permanent.

Being exposed to noise, including loud music, for a long time can also lead to hearing loss because the relentless sound wears down and destroys the cochlea's hair cells. This is a genuine problem for rock musicians, who often do suffer hearing loss. It's also a problem for anyone using headphones turned up too high, anyone whose hobbies include noisy vehicles such as motorcycles or snowmobiles, or those who work in a factory or on a construction job and don't see the point of wearing protective earplugs. The real danger here is that someone may think he or she has finally gotten used to the noise and not realize that the reason is that he or she has suffered a hearing loss.

CHAPTER FOUR

WHEN WE NEED HELP TO HEAR

In the past, there weren't many medical options for those with hearing issues. Throughout the nineteenth century, people would cup their hands under their ears to try to get more sound waves into the ear, or they could carry ear trumpets, which funneled amplified sound into the ear but literally looked like trumpets and were large, bulky, and not very effective. By the middle of the twentieth century, they could wear hearing aids, which were clumsy, noticeable, and not too efficient.

By the end of the twentieth century, all that had changed. Now, at beginning of the twenty-first century, there are four different types of hearing aids: conventional, programmable, digital, and disposable.

Modern hearing devices work with the physical components of the ear and the brain to help those with hearing loss.

TYPES OF HEARING AIDS

The conventional hearing aid is the most basic type, not too far advanced from earlier designs except for being smaller and less noticeable. Conventional hearing aids are made up of a microphone, an amplifier, and a receiver. The wearer of a conventional hearing aid can change the device's volume, louder or softer, but that's all. Any major changes mean getting the device altered at the factory. And that means being without it for several days.

A programmable hearing aid is a definite step forward. It is set and adjusted by computer to match the wearer's needs. A programmable device usually

Today, there are more types of hearing devices than ever, which can be easily disguised and work within the complex structure of the ear.

has an automatic volume control as well, so that the wearer doesn't need to worry about making adjustments. Any major changes can be made during a visit to the doctor's office.

The most modern version of the hearing aid is called the digital hearing aid. This is a totally new device that works with a computer chip that makes it programmable to very specific frequencies. It's called a digital hearing aid because it has a digital circuit that produces far clearer sound than the older hearing aids. It's still in the testing stage but looks very promising.

The fourth type of hearing aid, the disposable device, is meant to be used for only a few months, or until a wearer's needs change, and then replaced. It isn't as sophisticated as the digital device.

WEARING HEARING AIDS

There are also four different ways of wearing hearing aids. Completely-in-the-canal, or CIC, hearing aids fit neatly into the ear canal and are almost completely invisible. They aren't for anyone with the most severe hearing loss, or for children, whose ear canals are constantly growing with the rest of their bodies.

In-the-canal, or ITC, hearing aids are placed closer to the entrance of the ear canal and are more visible than CIC devices. In-the-ear, or ITE, hearing aids are placed at the entrance of the ear canal and are the most clearly visible. Behind-the-ear, or BTE, devices used to be fairly bulky and easily noticed. Modern

Modern hearing devices are designed to fit within the ear canal and be completely invisible, perhaps inspiring more people to use them.

technology has shrunk them, though they are still fairly noticeable. They can be dyed to match a user's natural skin tone.

REPAIRING DAMAGED HEARING

Will scientists ever be able to repair damaged hearing completely? It seems more and more likely. There are already some successful surgical techniques that can repair damage wherever possible and even bypass damage that's too great to repair.

Congenital microtia, the lack of an outer ear, is obviously something that's noticeable at a child's birth. Usually, surgery is postponed until the child is four or five years old. By this age, the ear structure is more fully grown but the child is still young enough to develop normal speech. The work is performed not by a doctor but by a plastic surgeon working in conjunction with the doctor.

Until recently, the structure of the new ear was taken from the cartilage of one of the patient's ribs. But new advances in chemistry and cell growth are beginning to eliminate the need for a second surgery. Scientists are already able to grow skin and cartilage in the laboratory. Skin happens to be particularly easy to grow in sheets and is already being used for skin grafts on burn victims. Since skin also grows swiftly, a few skin cells taken from a patient can be quickly grown into new sheets of skin that the victim's body won't reject.

In the process of building a new ear, a doctor would first take a few cells from the patient and grow them in a small sheet.

Repairing hearing damage may involve more than just the ear. It can also involve the brain and other surrounding regions.

The frame of the ear would be shaped out of laboratory-grown cartilage, also grown from the patient's cells, or from a polymer compound. Polymer is the term for a chain of molecules, such as polymer plastic. But our bodies produce polymer chains

UNDERSTANDING THE INNER EAR

Since the beginning of manned spaceflight, there has been an increasing interest among scientists in the workings of the inner ear. How does it function in weightlessness? How can an astronaut adjust to the lack of gravity to give him or her a sense of balance? There's no "up" or "down" in space, after all. But astronauts discovered that they would instinctively decide for themselves which was the "ceiling" and which the "floor" of the Space Shuttle and the International Space Station. The problem comes when astronauts return to Earth. Then their inner ears have to learn how to balance their bodies once again. The process of readjustment usually takes a day or two. But it's important for scientists to figure out how to keep the inner ear functioning properly on longer space missions, such as those to Mars.

of molecules as well. The sheet of skin would be grown onto the ear framework. Then the new ear would be grafted onto the patient's head, giving him or her a brand-new, perfectly natural-looking ear.

There is much more to the ear than meets the eye. It is a complex and versatile component of the human body.

The job of repairing the damage caused by congenital atresia, the lack of an ear canal, is more difficult. An outer ear can look perfectly normal, masking the trouble inside, and several states have begun ordering hearing tests for all babies. Examination of a child's ear through an accurate CT scan tells the doctor the

Hearing damage can occur in any of the three main parts of the ear: external (red), middle (blue), and the inner (yellow) regions.

severity of the inner ear's damage. If it seems likely to the doctor that the child will be able to hear if surgery is performed, a difficult operation follows. The surgeon has to pick precisely the right spot to drill through the bone so that he or she can create a working ear canal. Since exposed bone is subject to infection, the surgeon also has to do very delicate skin grafts to cover the new canal. Sometimes it's necessary to reconstruct the middle ear as well, mostly to properly position the three bones. But it's worth all the effort if the surgery is successful because then the ear can hear normally.

Sometimes, though, the structure of the ear can't be repaired. In a new technique, cochlear implants can be surgically implanted in the ear to bypass the damaged parts of the inner ear and directly activate the hearing nerve.

THE FUTURE OF HEARING

What will the future of the ear be like? Genetic problems such as hereditary deafness or congenital atresia will probably be eliminated within the century or at least bypassed with much more sophisticated computerized hearing aids. It seems likely that within the century total deafness, which can't be helped with conventional hearing devices, will be eliminated as well.

But what about the ear itself and the range of human hearing? Will we someday be able to hear into the higher frequencies like a dog or even a bat? While the genetic engineering may be possible, the basic structure of our hearing doesn't seem likely to change too much. The ear is a pretty effective device after all.

GLOSSARY

AURICLE The entire outer ear.

CARTILAGE A form of flexible connective tissue.

CONGENITAL ATRESIA Lacking an external ear canal.

CONGENITAL MICROTIA Genetic deformation of the outer ear, ranging from minor to complete absence of the outer ear.

DECIBEL A unit of sound (loudness) measurement.

EUSTACHIAN TUBE A tube that connects the middle ear and the pharynx.

EXTERNAL AUDITORY CANAL, EXTERNAL AUDITORY MEATUS Scientific names for the ear canal.

HELIX The curve of the outer ear.

INNER EAR The innermost part of the ear, containing the cochlea, which translates sound waves into signals to the brain, and the three semicircular canals that give the body its sense of balance.

MIDDLE EAR The section of the ear bounded by the tympanic membrane at one end and the inner ear at the other, and containing the ossicular chain.

OSSICULAR CHAIN The three bones of the middle ear, the malleus (hammer), the incus (anvil), and the stapes (stirrup).

OTITIS MEDIA The scientific term for the common ear infection.

PINNA The bendable portion of the outer ear.

POLYMER A chain of molecules.

TINNITUS A ringing or buzzing in the ear.

TYMPANIC MEMBRANE The eardrum, a thin membrane that vibrates when sound waves strike it.

FOR MORE INFORMATION

American Speech-Language-Hearing Association (ASHA)

2200 Research Boulevard

Rockville, MD 20850-3289

(301) 296-5700

Website: http://www.asha.org

With more than 173,000 members, ASHA is a leading association for audiology and speech-language pathology support.

Better Hearing Institute

1444 I Street NW, Suite 700

Washington, DC 20005

(800) 327-9355

Website: http://www.betterhearing.org

The Better Hearing Institute provides information to help hearing-loss sufferers better understand hearing loss, its causes, and consequences, and treatment options.

Canadian Hearing Society

271 Spadina Road

Toronto, ON M5R 2V3

(877) 347-3427

Website: http://www.chs.ca

The Canadian Hearing Society (CHS) is a leading provider of information regarding hearing loss and related conditions.

Harvard Stem Cell Institute

Nervous System Diseases Program/Hearing Loss

Bauer Building, Administrative Suite

7 Divinity Avenue

Cambridge, MA 02138

(617) 496-4050

Website: http://hsci.harvard.edu/hearing-loss-0

The mission of the Harvard Stem Cell Institute (HSCI) is to develop new ways to prevent and treat hearing loss by replacing audio-assistive devices with biologically based therapies that treat the cause of the disease by protecting or replacing lost cells in the ear.

Hearing Health Foundation

363 Seventh Avenue, 10th Floor

New York, NY 10001-3904

(212) 257-6140

Website: http://www.hhf.org

The Hearing Health Foundation (HHF) is the largest private funder of hearing research. Its mission is to prevent and cure hearing loss and tinnitus through groundbreaking research.

Hearing Loss Association of America

7910 Woodmont Avenue, Suite 1200

Bethesda, MD 20814

(301) 657-2248

Website: http://www.hearingloss.org

The Hearing Loss Association of America (HLAA) is the nation's leading organization representing people with hearing loss.

National Hearing Conservation Association (NHCA)

12011 Tejon Street, Suite 700

Westminster, CO 80234

(303) 224-9022

Website: http://www.hearingconservation.org

The mission of the NHCA is to prevent hearing loss due to noise and other environmental factors in all sectors of society.

National Institute on Deafness and Other Communication Disorders

U.S. Department of Health & Human Services

National Institutes of Health

31 Center Drive, MSC 2320

Bethesda, MD 20892-2320

(301) 496-7243

Website: http://www.nidcd.nih.gov

The mission of the National Institute on Deafness and Other Communication Disorders (NIDCD) is to support research in the normal and disordered processes of hearing, balance, taste, smell, voice, speech, and language.

Vestibular Disorders Association

5018 NE 15th Avenue

Portland, OR 97211

(800) 837-8428

Website: http://www.vestibular.org

The Vestibular Disorders Association provides information related to inner ear damage.

WEBSITES

Because of the changing nature of Internet links, Rosen Publishing has developed an online list of websites related to the subject of this book. This site is updated regularly. Please use this link to access the list:

http://www.rosenlinks.com/HB3D/Ear

FOR FURTHER READING

Bouton, Katherine. *Say Again? Why I—And 50 Million Other Americans—Can't Hear You.* New York, NY: Farrar, Straus & Giroux, 2013.

Cox, Trevor. *The Sound Book: The Science of the Sonic Wonders of the World.* New York, NY: W.W. Norton & Co., 2014.

Hammond, Monique E. *What Did You Say? An Unexpected Journey into the World of Hearing Loss.* Minneapolis, MN: Two Harbors, 2012.

Heller, Eric Johnson. *Why You Hear What You Hear: An Experiential Approach to Sound, Music, and Psychoacoustics.* Princeton, NJ: Princeton University Press, 2013.

Horowitz, Seth S. *The Universal Sense: How Hearing Shapes the Mind.* New York, NY: Bloomsbury, 2012.

Rissman, Rebecca. *Hearing.* Chicago, IL: Heinemann Library, 2010.

Rogers, Kara. *Ear, Nose, and Throat.* New York, NY: Britannica Educational Publishing, 2012.

Yost, William A. *Fundamentals of Hearing: An Introduction.* San Diego, CA: Academic, 2007.

INDEX

ABOUT THE AUTHORS

Nicholas Faulkner is a writer living in New York.

Josepha Sherman is a professional author and folklorist, with over forty books and 125 short stories and articles in print. She's an active member of the Authors Guild and the Science Fiction Writers of America.

PHOTO CREDITS

Designer: Brian Garvey; Editor: Nicholas Croce;
Photo Researcher: Karen Huang